Healed

My Journey

By

Linda Raleigh Lane

Copyright ©2016; 2021 Linda Raleigh Lane

All rights reserved. No part of this publication may be reproduced, distributed, or transmitted in any form or by any means, including photocopying, recording, or other electronic or mechanical methods, without the prior written permission of the publisher, except in the case of brief quotations embodied in critical reviews and certain other noncommercial uses permitted by copyright law.

The King James Version of the Holy Bible is in the Public Domain.

American Standard Version (ASV) of the Holy Bible was first published in 1901 is in the Public Domain.

Scripture quotations taken from the Amplified® Bible (AMP), Copyright © 2015 by The Lockman Foundation Used by permission. www.Lockman.org

Scripture quotations are from The Holy Bible, English Standard Version® (ESV®), copyright © 2001 by Crossway, a publishing ministry of Good News Publishers. Used by permission. All rights reserved.

Bible text from the Good News Translation is not to be reproduced in copies or otherwise by any means except as permitted in writing by American Bible Society, 1865 Broadway, New York, NY 10023 (www.americanbible.org).

Scripture taken from The Message. Copyright © 1993, 1994, 1995, 1996, 2000, 2001, 2002. Used by permission of NavPress Publishing Group.

ISBN- 978-1-951300-07-4

Liberation's Publishing – West Point - Mississippi

Healed

My Journey

Foreword

Though each of our lives will at some point and time be touched by death, we can never get used to the idea. Living and dying are part of the same cycle. Living is part of dying just like dying is part of living. It cannot be escaped. It's always there, yet we do not want to be reminded of it or see it headed our way. Even more so, there is no consolation in the words one often hears after losing a loved one, "They are with the Lord. They are in a better place."

We often hear and say, "I know where my loved one is. They are not in the grave. They are gone to be with the Lord." As hard as we try to remind ourselves of these "Christian Truths" they do not take away the pain or the sight of the casket our loved one is laid to rest in. We want them back! We want them here with us in this realm.

The last place we see their body is in a casket. Their remains laid in their individual box. A connection is made, and we are in love with the remains. Even though the spirit is no longer there, the body that housed that spirit is what we're left with. Once buried, we can no longer touch the remains. We miss the remains! It's so hard to let go of the remains. In our mind we reason, "If we let go of the remains, we let go of the person." I suppose this is why cremation is good for some, because they can choose to take the remains home. They can choose the right place to set their loved ones other than a cemetery.

No one goes to a cemetery just to look at the grass, no matter how beautiful it is. No one just joyrides through to see the beautiful bouquets of flowers. We go because it is the last spot we saw and made contact with the remains. Over time the remnants of the flowers fade away, not just by the weather, by people as well. Some may think you hold on too long. That place where our loved one remains are; remains in our hearts forever. We don't mind buying a headstone for it, or even putting their names on said headstone. We bring balloons and flowers to that place where the remains and headstone are.

While yet living we buy a headstone with our name on it and place it next to our deceased loved one. We find contentment by marking our place beside our loved one. This consoles us somehow, knowing that our remains will be next to theirs. Our final resting place on earth will be together.

As a child of God and a mother I know that my son, Benjamin, is in heaven. I know that heaven and hell are real. But I also know that my son did not touch or see the latter. His father and I can only take credit for bringing him up in the fear of the Lord. Benjamin, by his own confession of faith took the necessary steps to secure his place in eternity with the Lord. He was taught well and obeyed. I can joyfully say, "Thank you God for Jesus!" My son is in the hands of the Lord.

We know that we cannot live forever on this side, but the loss of a love one can be a very devastating time. As a mother, I can say when you lose a child it's like the unbiblical cord is severed all over again. There is a hole left in you that nothing can fill. No, it is not like when I gave birth to him. There is no womb or afterbirth. There is a different sense of loss. The child God gave me to protect and nourish is no longer there, but my mind has not processed that. He's supposed to be here, but he is not. I still have nourishment for him that he can no longer receive, I have a covering for him that is vacant. These things I have for him, but nowhere to lay them down. The connection is lost, and now the attachment is gone. Where did it go?

The safety net is broken. You realize that what they needed from you was also needed by you. No one can fill the empty space. The love I have for him has no place to go, and the love he gave me no longer flows to me. Not only has he left without me, but he has also left me open, unprotected, alone, and without a covering for the empty hole inside of me.

Revelations 14:13 tells us, "Then I heard [the distinct words of] a voice from heaven, saying," Write, 'Blessed (happy, prosperous, to be admired) are the dead who die in the Lord from now on!" "Yes, [blessed indeed]," says the Spirit, "so that they may rest and have relief from their labors, for their deeds do follow them." (AMP) Thank you Lord! I had to use these words to comfort myself as I comforted others. I pray this comforts you!

Preface

As her pastor, I watched Linda allow her faith to become the anchor for her soul as she and her family faced her son's Benjamin's death. She was able, in spite of what she was facing to comfort others while being healed herself. Not only was she able to find the help she needed but allowed God to transform her pain into a ministry for the body of Christ.

This book has renewed my faith that in Christ no part of our lives is wasted, especially not our pain. I applaud Linda for allowing God to use perhaps the worst circumstance any parent could ever face to become a road map for others who will inevitably face a similar fate. God never promised we would not have trying circumstances, but that He would give us victory in all of our afflictions. This book captures how the love of God, and the peace of His presence gives the believer the grace to bring glory to God regardless of our circumstances.

I appreciate her bravery and perseverance as well as her desire to help others. This book is a powerful illustration that God is faithful to perform His word; therefore, this book is a must read for anyone facing the death of a loved one.

Thank you, Linda, for sharing your journey from pain to victory!

-Pastor Steve Jamison

Healed: My Journey

Table of Content

Foreword v

Preface ix

From Death to Life 13

We Still See You 17

Floating on the Clouds 18

Straight From a Mother's Heart 21

Straight From a Father's Heart 29

The Journey 31

My Journey Begins 35

The Death Blow and The Awakening 47

Coming to Myself 65

How Do I Make It? 71

How Did I Get There? 81

Where Do I Go From Here? 89

Special Acknowledgements 95

Healed: My Journey

From Death to Life

I remember my husband; Thomas and I were driving home from church one Sunday afternoon. It was such a beautiful day. He saw me looking through the windshield and while looking at me he could see the tears filling up in my eyes. The tears started to fall so he asked me if I was thinking of Benjamin. I nodded my head, "yes" and I told him a revelation that I had just received from the Lord.

There is a saying that is placed on a lot of obituaries that say, "Our Loss is Heaven's Gain!" I looked at him with a smile on my face and said to him, "Who says it's a loss?" If the Lord giveth, then the Lord can take away. Death now is something that I see very differently since my son passed away. In the book of 1 John 3:14 it states, "We know that we have passed out of death into Life, because we love the brothers and sisters. He who does not love remains in [Spiritual] death."

A friend of mine, Pastor R. H. Brown told me one day that death is the last trial of your life. However, if you die in the Lord the trial turns into eternity. Today our loved ones who die in the Lord are no longer facing a trial, but an opportunity to spend eternity with the Lord and that is what we want. Oftentimes when someone passes away one of the first questions, we want to ask is how old were they? Or what was wrong with them? Our flesh is more concerned with the outward man rather than the inward man. We must come to the place where we can concentrate on the fact that the individual was saved. It is not about the condition that they were in but the position they were in because that is what gets us through in the end. The consolation of knowing in your spirit that the individual was ready to meet Jesus is enough to keep going.

Through this book I am living my life from the past, to the present and through the future. I am not only able to tell this story, but I am living it! Jesus has been strength! My hope is that you the reader, will carry with you a renewed sense of an awakening in life, and that although death is real, know that there is also life after death. I have discovered that sometimes there is life in death. Although it could have taken me out mentally, spiritually as well as physically, God had other ideas in mind. When this journey started out, God himself was my life jacket to hold me and pull me back to shore. He did not just pump out the water that was not needed, but He gave me new water. It was not just to breathe with, but it saved my life and now I am a new creature.

If you are having trouble with grief, these words are not intended to pass judgement on you. For me, there was no time limit on my grief. There was no right or wrong way for me to grieve. I was told what things I should do and the things I should not do. I was not able to go to counseling, but God led me through His way. Through His way, I am healed. My journey does not mean that there are no other solutions to dealing with the pain or regrets. It does not mean that everything is perfect. It is not, but I know who to give the hurt to. I am not alone. God loves me, and I am healthy in my way of thinking. It took me years to get to this place, but I thank God for the path that led me to knowing where I was, where I am and where I am headed.

I wanted to say to anyone who has experienced the death of a family member, the pain can be excruciating but also bearable in the Lord. Furthermore, when a child passes on it is different from the death of anyone else. It does not matter how many people say that they know how you feel, if they have not buried a child, they cannot understand the depth of your pain. Only God can really heal that hurt.

Healed: My Journey

Linda Raleigh Lane

We Still See You

We still see you, in the eyes of your dad,
You tried to walk like him when you were a lad.
You grew up into a teen,
but to your mother you would cling.
You loved spending time with sister;
there were only things the two of you could share, Big
Brother didn't mind protecting you;
His height wasn't the only thing that was there.
But you left us from deeper depths to higher heights with a
smile on your face,
and your hand extended to God.
You left us with memories that will forever live in our
hearts.
You will never be gone nor forgotten
for in the eyes of each one of us,
We still see you.

Floating on the Clouds

Way up high in the clear blue sky,

I told you where I was and where I am;

I'm not far away, for I am floating on the clouds every day.

It all seems like a breath and a heartbeat away, yes close to you and I will forever stay.

Why would I leave you?

You know where I told you I would be,

I see you looking up at me;

Sometimes just to see the expression on your face,

I can tell you are also amazed.

I'm floating on the clouds;

and you are on the ground,

But there is no separation between the loves that has always been found.

We see the same things

but I'm able to reach out and touch them

and you're able to touch them too,

because God is opening your eyes and heart to see him too,

You are growing not without me I know,

because I help you in ways that others don't realize or know how to show.

The clouds come together in such a grand way,

all kinds of shapes and sizes in many different ways.

They dance across the sky God prepared and his hands have made,

Not only for your eyes to behold but will also touch a soul.

There are clouds in the sky and some even at night,

and I float at that time too.

My favorite color I see up here are orange, white, and blue.

Looking over the heavens now up, down, and around to see such a beautiful, glorious sight,

The awesomeness of God is surrounding me.

I no longer need the helicopter and I have no need for a plane or jet.

Just look at the cotton balls, why they are the whitest ones yet;

God is here! I told you that I made it safe, and now I would not want to leave this place. This is not farewell or goodbye.

I'm smiling and watching you because;

I'm floating on the clouds in the sky.

Healed: My Journey

Straight From a Mother's Heart

I was blessed with three children; that is how many I birthed into life. I love them all beyond measure. Benjamin just happened to be the one that got away from us too soon. I love all three of my children equally, and for the sake of this story I will tell you more about Benjamin's life and the role he played in bringing so much joy to God's earth before he passed on. I can remember the numerous times my son Benjamin and I watched his favorite holiday tv show, *The Wizard of Oz*.

I'm not sure if it was the story line of how Dorothy was trying to get home or the story line of one of her companions that he loved. It could have been the lion who thought he wasn't brave but was. It could have been the Tin Man who wanted a heart not knowing he had the biggest heart of them all. Last but not least it could have been the scarecrow who in search of a brain did not realize that he was the thinker of the group. Whatever the reason, Benjamin loved The Wizard of Oz.

One thing I will always treasure is a conversation I had with someone I met. This man told me that he would go to this place of business often. Every time he saw this particular young man at work in that place of business, he would be smiling. He was always smiling. The man went on to say that no matter how bad he was feeling after speaking to the young man he would feel better. There was just something about the young employee. The man would leave with a smile on his face.

As our conversation progressed, the man went on to say he was sorry to hear my son had passed away. He told me he didn't know my son. I told him my son's name. He didn't recognize it and said again he didn't know him. We continued to talk, I told him more about Benjamin and that's when he put two and two together. "Wait a minute. That's your son!" He exclaimed. "I didn't know that. I talked to him all of the time." He could not believe we were talking about the same person.

That's the kind of person Benjamin was, he always made others feel better just by being in their presence. He seemed to understand the value of a hug, and he didn't mind showing his love to me openly in public; he supported me whole heartedly, loved me thoroughly and unconditionally. He was a very protective mama's boy.

I miss you now and I will miss and love you forever. I think of you, and I know that you are my angel watching over me. Thank you, Benjamin for being my baby, my son and being by my side.

As I said earlier, God blessed me with three wonderful

children. In addition to Benjamin, there is Crystal. Crystal is like the second mother with her pampering qualities. She's always trying to help, correct, and give advice, but will quickly remind my husband and I and her brothers how she helped to take care of them, the boys, changing diapers and all. She wanted to be known as the big sister gorgeous one, smart and the oldest, she was worthy of the respect she demanded.

Jon has the quality of strength, determined to be the strong silent type. He hovered over them all and would make them feel intimidated because of his height. He loves to make everyone feel good by laughing. He is strong willed or what Crystal and Ben called stubborn. Benjamin was meticulous about who he was, who he portrayed, and how all of us made him look whenever we went out. He brought a picture of balance to the family. He was definitely a mama's boy and did not care who knew it. He could be serious minded but loved to laugh too. and make everyone pay attention.

One day when they were all together, while I'm in the next room I caught a conversation between the three of them.

Ben stated to Jon, "Boy, you know you're adopted?"

"Naw man!" Jon replied.

"Yeah you are." Crystal chimed in.

Jon looked at her, but she had a solemn look on her face. Ben said it again, "You are adopted!"

"You are the youngest, where did you get that from?" Jon reasoned.

"Mama told me, Her and daddy found you on the road for real, I'm sorry but I had to tell you brother, you know you act a little different than we do." Benjamin still keeping up the game. "Ask Crystal."

Jon looking at the expression on Crystal's face knew the two of them must be planning something. Jon got really quiet because it seemed to be working. Jon sat down and everything was quiet. Benjamin and Crystal could not hold their composure any longer. They burst out laughing. Jon did not laugh. He did finally give them a slight smile. "I knew what you were doing." He stated. "I just played along." The whole family had the biggest laugh about it even now.

Benjamin was not only the baby boy and mama's boy; but he knew how to minister grace to me in the simplest form and out of a courteous goodwill, but my husband stated that he could see him preaching the gospel to so many people. Sometimes it is like a dream, because there are days that I still cannot believe he is gone, and I look around where there are so many things in and around our home that remind me of him. The room that was once his bedroom, that held the

pictures he painted; the ones that he crafted from his heart but drew with his hands, down to the trash can that he built with his name carved into it. He left his mark on all of us, in us and somehow that same mark is still conditioning us.

He ministered to me in a very special way on May 1, 2011 when I had the opportunity to preach my first public message from the Lord by being there for me; I did not go to the morning service, and he thought it would be best if he stayed with me so that he could "attend " to me until it was time to leave to go to the church, I stayed in my room so I could meditate, read, and pray and Benjamin was there every step of the way to make sure that I had what I needed; he would often come to the door and knock to see if I was okay, if I needed water or anything else. When he gave the final knock, I knew it was time to go and he said "Ma, are you ready?" because he was my driver. That day he made sure I got my bible, water, a towel, and comfortable shoes. I was nervous, and he could see it, but before I could utter it out loud, he said "Ma, you're going to do good".

He put me in the car, shut my door, made sure I was comfortable, and drove without the radio on knowing the value of peace and quiet that we both thought I needed, so with determination and care we rode in silence, and every so often he would look over at me smile and ask, "are you alright Ma"? When I look back sometimes, I wish that we had engrossed ourselves in conversation, but the way that he ministered to me that day not only spoke to my heart but also to his character.

I know that this book was not written to give Benjamin's story, but he was the catalyst that God used to capture what I needed to survive and to prepare for what's next; to do better at hearing from God, listening to God and being able to apply healing to others lives the way it has been given to me, for healing and forgiveness in the hearts of others. Healing has been my journey, and it will continue to be because I have walked away with a sense of healing all around me, from my heart, mind, and my spirit. I have been set free, that's what forgiveness will do. John 8:36 AMP says

So if the Son makes you free, then you are unquestionably free. Benjamin is and so am I!   "Not only is Healed My Journey, but My Journey is Healed"

Healed: My Journey

Straight From a Father's Heart

Benny Hinn is the nickname I called my son. There are days I still can't believe he's gone, simply because I miss that boy so much. I often think, if he was here, what would he be doing? He was smart, clean cut, neat, and handsome.

Sometimes we never come to know why or how God allows things to happen, but in his infinite wisdom it happened for God's glory and for our good. Even I questioned God and cried out to him, "God! Why my baby? Why my son?" But God spoke to me and said, "that's my son too." And yes, I know that God's will has to be done. Satan has no authority! He is God's devil, and he can only do what God allows. Therefore, if God don't allow it, Satan can't bring it to pass. Sometimes what we consider a tragedy it is not like that with the Lord. *Psalm 116:15(KJV) says Precious in the sight of the Lord is the death of his saints.* We cannot afford to take our eyes off of God. I know in my spirit that Benjamin is with the Lord. I will always remember him. God allowed me to be his father for the time he gave him to me, and for that I am grateful. He chose me to be his daddy in the earth.

Healed: My Journey

The Journey

These passages of scripture are not just words on a page, but were spoken to me by God and are also found in Isaiah 61:2-3

"to comfort all who mourn, to grant to those who mourn in Zion the following: To give them a turban instead of dust [on their heads, a sign of mourning], The oil of joy instead of mourning, The garment [expressive] of praise instead of a disheartened spirit. So they will be called the trees of righteousness [strong and magnificent, distinguished for integrity, justice, and right standing with God] the planting of the Lord, that He may be glorified. (AMP)

"to comfort all that mourn; To appoint unto them that mourn in Zion, to give unto them beauty for ashes, the oil of joy for mourning, the garment of praise for the spirit of heaviness, that they might be called trees of righteousness, the planting of the LORD, that he might be glorified." (KJV)

"to comfort all who mourn; to grant to those who mourn in Zion--- to give them a beautiful headdress instead of ashes, the oil of gladness instead of mourning, the garment of praise instead of a faint spirit; that they may be called oaks of righteousness, the planting of the Lord, that he may be glorified. (ESV)

"to comfort all who mourn, To care for the needs of all

who mourn in Zion, give them bouquets of roses instead of ashes, Messages of joy instead of news of doom, a praising heart instead of a languid spirit. Rename them "Oaks of Righteousness" planted by God to display his glory. (MSG)

"He has sent me to comfort all who mourn, To give to those who mourn in Zion Joy and gladness instead of grief, A song of praise instead of sorrow. They will be like trees That the Lord himself has planted. They will all do what is right, And God will be praised for what he has done. (GNT)

"to comfort all that mourn; to appoint unto them that mourn in Zion, to give unto them a garland for ashes, the oil of joy for mourning, the garment of praise for the spirit of heaviness; that they may be called trees of righteousness, the planting of Jehovah, that he may be glorified." (ASV)

This is my ministry; what I have been assigned to do. I have been made aware of what I am to do in this life, and it is an awesome thing. I will speak to others as I am being spoken to by God. I have been given an opportunity to reach out, so that my life would reflect my creator. I am to give what's given to me and to do his bidding. An exchange is to take place; I can stand in the gap and offer to others what has been offered to me.

I extend the invitation. There is always a better way if we choose to be a part of it. I don't always have to accept what it looks like or feels like. I just have to do it God's way and my way will be made. I can have beauty instead of ashes; I can have gladness instead of mourning. I have been given an avenue, and I can also offer the same to another.

The call of God on my life took a turn for me and brought me to this place. What God called me to do for others is what he did for me. I want to give hope; it does not have to be the end. It can be a beginning, a step up, a glimpse of light, a shredding of the old to awaken the new. It can be an exchange of the impossible for the possible. I never knew that could be possible with my life, yet here I am living the journey!

Being healed implies that I am in a different place than where I was before. One thing was being brought to an end. The conclusion of something that once was and now is no more. I am sound and made healthy. Being healed says that I once was bound and blind, but now I'm free and I can see. I never thought that my spiritual eyes would be opened this way!

Healed is a place that we all try to get too. Before healing takes place, we may find ourselves going other places along the way.

Before	After
Healed is far from God	Healed is a safe place
Healed is sad	Healed is happiness
Healed is doubting	Healed is believing
Healed is the same	Healed is different
Healed is afraid	Healed is fearless
Healed is resentful	Healed is pleasing
Healed is distraught	Healed is calm
Healed is hopeless	Healed is joyfulness
Healed is torn apart	Healed is complete
Healed is confusion	Healed is peace

My Journey Begins

I realize there are some things in this life that we can do nothing about. We have no control over. Thank God there is, because just think of how big a mess we would make. Change is hard to deal with. You expect things to remain the same because you are already comfortable. You get accustomed to things that you know and never want them to change.

People will say, well! That's all a part of life. Even so, you don't expect life to happen to you. God gave me the best parents, not just in the world, but the ones he knew that I needed for my good. Robert Lee Raleigh and Lucy Mae, they both took the time to mold me in the ways of God without me even knowing it. I really didn't know that they were grooming me to follow them as they followed Christ.

My dad taught me that I could take money from men at an early age! Not like you think! My mother, well, although I was afraid of her like many others. I respected what she stood for. The strength that she wore, the values she upheld, all traits of a leader. My mother was a very strong influence in my life. I have not always seen it that way, but the more that I matured I understood.

I just didn't want to look like her or act like her in my younger years, but it's too late now. I thank God for the ways of my father and my mother. I thank Him for the hard lessons that I learned as a child. Oh, and not just me. If you ever meet or have ever met Robert JR, Lee Earnest, and Dorothy Jean, you came in contact with Robert Lee and Lucy Mae. Since I am the baby, I never let them forget it. Here I am now. I did begin as Linda Kay Raleigh and journeyed from there to where I am now. The same person, just more mature.

I was going to school and every day it was an adventure. Singing in chorus, and singing in class, my teachers would have me to sing all of the time. They would sometimes come and get me out of class to just go across the hall and sing. I believe they all found out I could sing from my music teacher, Mrs. Jones. I came all the way from "I'm a little teapot" to "Without God I can't do nothing" What a place!

I know that healing is what we all need in every area and every aspect of our lives; it is a process that takes time. It also implies that damage has been done. There is hurt and pain that has left open wounds. It doesn't matter if the healing we need comes is from situations or circumstances. It doesn't matter if they are self-inflicted, or from life itself. We all want to recover.

Jeremiah 17:14 says, *"Heal me, O Lord, and I will be healed; Save me and I will be saved, for you are my praise.*

(AMP) I know the only way out is through, but sometimes the way through is also down. This can happen to all of us.

I can remember the very first time I experienced the physical healing power of God. One beautiful summer afternoon my husband Thomas and I were at home doing some yard work. All of a sudden, I became very ill. for someone that seemed to be doing great, sickness grabbed a whole of my body and fear latched on. I became weak to the point I fainted and fell down on the ground. My husband was still on the lawn mower, so I had to try and get his attention. I tried calling out his name and waving my hands at him. He couldn't even see or hear me from the place where he was. Many of you know it seems like forever when you are the one that is in need. Amen!

My husband finally noticed me, and something was wrong! I couldn't call his name out anymore. I was too weak, tired, hot, and exhausted. I could see him coming towards me. He got me inside the house. I was leaning on him every step of the way. He finally got me to the bed; I was so weak.

Someone may say that I just stayed outside too long. I got too hot or had a heat stroke, but my husband Thomas, the first thing he did was start praying! He didn't take me to a clinic or to the emergency room. He simply prayed for me. Jesus says in Matthew 18:20, *"For where two or three are gathered in My name [meeting together as My followers], I am there among them."* (AMP) We both touched and agreed there is nothing better for a Christian today than to think to pray FIRST.

He sat there on the side of the bed and prayed, talked to me, and prayed some more. He stopped all of a sudden and said, "Lynn I feel impressed of the Lord to call Sis. Gloria, Evangelist Gloria Jamison." Now, I know we already knew each other being in the same church together, but this was going to be different.

Sister Gloria was going to be invited to my home. We would no longer just be church members together. I would see her not just as a minister of the gospel, teacher, prayer warrior and intercessor, but she actually would be coming to pray and intercede on my behalf. She would also know something about me! She would see inside my house, both of them; the physical one and the spiritual one.

Nevertheless, my husband called, and she came. I remember her walking into the bedroom. She started to ask me a question, "how are you doing sister?" I remember saying that I was not feeling well. This question was a whole lot easier to ask than to answer. I felt awful, drained, and weak. Everything around me seemed as if it was far off because I could not focus.

I just wanted to close my eyes. Jesus was all I could say, because everything ached. James 5:14-15 says, *"Is anyone among you sick? He must call for the elders (spiritual leaders) of the church and they are to pray over him, anointing him with oil in the name of the Lord; and the prayer of faith will restore the one who is sick, and the Lord will raise him up; and if he has committed sins, he will be forgiven."* (AMP)

Sister Gloria faith (belief without need of proof) agreed with my husband faith, anointed me with oil and began to pray powerfully together. All I could say was, "Jesus, Jesus, Jesus!" The word of God, power of prayer and belief (acceptance of the truth) were in line together. So much so, that I gained strength and begin to thank God for my healing. I got up off my bed and walked down my hallway.

I felt sick to my stomach, lightheaded, and nauseous. I ran into the bathroom. This did not stop the persistent woman of God. The enemy wasn't trying to let go and the God in her wasn't either. She came into the bathroom with me, laying her hands on me and praying. This all while I was on my knees in front of the toilet. Gloria Jamison said to me, that's alright sister, you're healed!

I did not know then that Jehovah was not only the God that healed thee, but that day he became the God that healed me. "Without God, I can do nothing" this song was more real to me than it had been before.

For me singing was never a problem, but I didn't understand what the words meant as a young girl. I didn't know what they were doing to me. I loved to sing I actually received joy from it, even though I didn't know why. Now as a recording artist and a minister I have come to realize that my dad and my mom were my manager and producer.

They began to cultivate in me what God had already given them for me. I can remember so vividly on Sunday afternoons after church, my dad would have me to sing. The deacons would be outside under the shade tree sitting in the circle with their crisp white shirts, suspenders, and each one of them had on a hat. Mom would be in the kitchen frying chicken, and you could smell the aroma through the screen door. Daddy would say, "come on baby girl and sing for us."

He loved to hear me sing, and it made him so proud! I would get in the middle of the circle, using a stick as my microphone and sing. Afterwards daddy would instruct one of the men to take their hat off, pass it around, and raise my baby an offering. They would too! (That's how I learned how to take money from men at an early age) I was always so excited, even though I never got any of the money! But maybe I did. I did get a chance to go to school, eat chicken, have a place to sleep and a bed to sleep in. I also had the clothes that my mom made for me and my sister. What an example of love shown to me.

When my father passed away, I remembered specific details of riding the tractor with him. I was always glad about that. Because he let me ride on his lap. I remember when he taught me how to tie my shoes. I kept telling him that I couldn't do it, but he spanked me every time I told him that. I finally got it right. I endured the switch. It didn't take as long as I thought it would.

When he was about to leave me, I knew something different was happening. He was in the hospital in Memphis, Tennessee and children were not allowed in the hospital as visitors. I did not see him and then one day they told us that we could see him, I was so afraid. I wanted to see my daddy but when we got to the hospital, as a little girl, this place was big, cold, and scary and everyone I saw wore white and they were whispering as if they all had a secret. I had not seen my daddy for a long time but even one night to a little girl is a long time to be away from her daddy. When we walked into daddy's room I remember someone picking me up to set me on the side of his bed, I did not say anything I just looked at him, he looked at me and placed his hands over mine and held onto them tightly and he said baby girl! but I did not say anything, I know he looked different, but he sounded the same, like my hero, and that was the last time I saw him alive, he did not come back home again. I never stopped singing.

Daddy was gone and I felt as if I was all alone. No one else was cheering me on or encouraging me, telling me that I did good. I was daddy's little singing bird. After his passing it was as if mama was on a mission. She started to make me practice singing at home in another room in front of the chifforobe with a comb. I used it as a microphone in front of the mirror. (I had moved up, from a stick to a comb).

Mama wanted me to know that singing for the Lord was serious and she was instructional. She told me that I was not supposed to run down the aisle singing. Don't get up and tell people that I was going to attempt to sing a song. Just sing. I really thought she had eyes in the back of her head or x-ray vision. I didn't like being in front of that mirror. Every time I would move away, she would say, "get back in front of the mirror!" I would look around and see if there was a camera or hole somewhere, but I never saw anything.

My mother would take me to revival services at different churches and tell the Pastors, "Call my baby up to sing!" And they would do just that. She didn't say to me verbally that she was pleased or that I did a good job. I knew.

She would not have taken me to those churches or taught me about singing. When I would be called up to sing, I wasn't sure if it was out of fear or respect. My mother was an outspoken person, and even though some of the young people seem to be afraid of her sometimes, she was respected for being who she was. She meant what she said and said what she meant.

I continued to love singing as I grew up; from a child, the Lord saved me! I accepted him and began to have a different outlook. It wasn't just talent, even though singing came easy for me. I began to be particular in the songs that I would sing. I began to pray that God would use me to bless someone else. I didn't just want to be singing to others. I began to think to myself, "Is this what mama and daddy saw in me?" I wanted others to get something out of my singing. I wanted them to have an experience that would be unforgettable!

During this time, I was growing up. Not only was I maturing. I was getting a little bolder. Not to the point that Lucy Mae would get a piece of my mind. If I did, I wouldn't be here today. I was getting confident. I can remember at a revival one night. I was called up to sing and mama said (out loud), "sing my favorite song." To this day I have no idea why my mouth flew open, but when it did, out came "Mama,

I will sing your song when we get home."

Now! I had said it, even more so, I know she heard those words too. I couldn't take them back! No matter how I tried or would have wanted too. I thought I was in trouble, but to my surprise she did not say anything then or when we got home. Mama never said a word about it, and I began to wonder why she did not mention it on the ride home, it was as if she had not spoken it to me at all, because it was so unlike her to let something go when I had promised to do it. I believe she already knew the impact of what I had said to her and how it would affect me so much so that her silence spoke more to me than any words she could have said.

Linda, being called into the ministry! I said Linda (me). I was already singing praises unto God lifting up his name, praying and worshipping. So, no not my God, did I hear you call me? Not one, now two times, but maybe I just don't know the voice of God when I hear it. I am married to a Pastor, but this is not a time to ask family, my husband, or my children if this is a good idea or what kind of preacher would I be?

I know in my spirit and through the word that God was talking to me. And it was no longer my choice whether I wanted to or not. At the moment I knew that I had to do something, I was uncomfortable and scared. I thank God for my Pastors Steve and Loren Jamison for guidance. Their prayers and direction, reminding me that it was not about me. I was thinking how unprepared I was and that I was not capable enough. They listened intently as I spoke to them what was so heavy on my heart.

My husband seemed to grasp every word that I said in such a way that it seemed as if he had heard it for the very first time. I assumed I had an excuse because I was already ministering in song. My Pastor stated to me that the Gospel must be preached! Then he said something that got my attention and scared me all at the same time. He said souls were tied to me, and they were waiting to hear the word from me!

Like they were assigned to ME! Now what could I say that had not already been said? Nevertheless, God won, and I delivered the word he gave me on May 1, 2011, *Come out of darkness into light* with a subtopic - *From sin to salvation*. A young lady gave her heart to God. He had spoken.

Healed: My Journey

The Death Blow and The Awakening

As I stated at the beginning of my book, everyone's life will at some point be touched by the death of a loved one. They may pass away young, old, through sickness, or just unexpectedly. I not only faced going down that road, but I had to walk down that road with the passing of my youngest son Benjamin. It was not just a place that I went. God brought me back and saved me. The passing of my son left me with more than just a thought, but this message.

It also showed me how to see God in a way that I never knew existed. Through this ordeal, I learned of God and was able to see my son at the same time. In preaching my first public message May 1, 2011, and my son passing away May 28, 2011. Thinking of this as a memory, Memorial Day weekend now took on a whole new meaning.

I began to question myself. If I had heard from God to be called into the ministry and chosen for this great task. Why hadn't I told my son not to drive? Why hadn't I seen this coming? I must not have been focusing on what I should have been doing for the Lord. I knew what I could not do, and that seemed to be nothing. I was lost with no hope, and no way out. I couldn't explain it. Who wants to know that I can't cope? I am supposed to sing now and preach. No one else is going to understand is all I could think.

When God gave us our baby boy, he also gave us his name Benjamin, meaning "son of my right hand" but in the Samaritan Pentateuch it means "Son of my days." His middle name Daniel meaning "God is my judge." I knew that something was very special about this boy He had allowed me to carry and care for. Yes, he was a mama's boy, and I would not have had it any other way. Not a perfect son; but he was my son.

I remember the very night he accepted Christ as his Lord and savior and gave his heart to God. We were not in a youth service or at the church, but in our room at home.

I remember him crying so. I do not know who cried more amongst the three of us. I do remember being so astonished that he was ready and the fact that he wanted to. I saw his life take on the shape of a very attentive and caring young man. He was precise in his ways and loved the company of himself while making things with his hands. I did not mind that because he drew pictures for me and of me. He was always faithful to something if he wanted to do it.

I remember when he wanted to learn how to play the drums. His father found him a drum teacher and he learned quickly and started to play for the church. He wanted to know how to play the keyboard; so, after he got himself a job; he saved up money to buy him one and taught himself how to play. The confidence and determination of what he could do proved to his dad that he not only earned the right to mow the yard with the riding mower but could handle responsibility. He even let him drive his Mercedes to his senior prom.

Crystal and Jon could not wrap their heads around that one because they had never drove it. They wondered how did that happen? He was always a very careful driver. It was so funny. I could ride with him without holding on to the door handle or top of the car and be so comfortable. I think he was being cautious so he would not hurt Susie (his little blue Lexus) rather than me. He loved that car, and to think they left here together.

The night before my son left us, I wasn't feeling well. It wasn't with a cold, stomach, fever, or a headache but a stiffness in my back. It caused a lot of pain all the way across to my shoulders. The next morning when I woke up that pain seemed to have spread to all of my upper body. My husband rubbed my shoulders, neck and massaged my upper back. At one point I told him I felt like I had been in an accident, because I was in such pain.

Once I got up, I saw that, Benjamin washed (Susie) his car off, and fixed himself breakfast. The two of us talked for a while. He wanted specific bed linen on his bed. He helped me pull them out before he got ready to leave for his haircut.

My husband and I were sitting out under the tree, as he was leaving. Benjamin said he would see us later and that he would be back to get ready for work. He waved up with the pointing of his finger, as he backed out of the driveway. He blew his car horn three times. He did this every time he left home. *I would not see Benjamin alive after that day.* I asked him once why he blew the horn like he did? He said, "one for the Father, one for the Son, and one for the Holy Ghost." That seemed odd to me, a young man being so concerned about spiritual things. At the same time, it also seemed right.

Nevertheless, he drove off to get his haircut. I remember it like it was yesterday Saturday May 28th. The phone rang at 2:51 pm. As I got closer to see who was calling a smile came across my face as I saw that it was him. I wondered what he had forgotten. I said, "Hello." But he did not say anything on the other end. I said "Hello." again, but still nothing. Another phone call followed at 3:17 to let me know there had been an accident on the highway and my son was in it.

I did not have the consciousness in my mind to even think to ask where on the highway? But instead, I hung the phone up and ran and told my husband. I did not know where. I did think how did the person know to call us? How did they get our number? Immediately I went into a daze. I did not know if it was real. But when I walked back to the kitchen the phone rang again snapping me back into reality. The person began to tell me where the accident had taken place. They informed me to not go there but meet the ambulance at the hospital.

Months later I was reminded about the phone call from my baby. Everyone thought I was exaggerating, but I believed he called me to say goodbye. After his phone was given to us, I took it to the cell phone carrier. They verified that the phone had indeed called me. My number was automatically dialed. I was the last person he had called. All I could say was, "Lord Help me!" But also, like Ben, And the *"Wizard of Oz"*, I knew that *"there is no place like home"* and not just this one, but the heavenly one.

May 28, 2011 is what I called "The Day". It was a day of awakening and a day of closings in my life. That day cut me through and through and tore my heart out. I died, and it did not seem to matter. I no longer cared. It was as if I no longer existed. I thought that I was the only one experiencing this deep agonizing pain that would not go away. At the same time, it didn't seem real.

I had a detective come to see me and say he had been assigned to the case. This was news to me because I did not realize that it was a case. He went on to tell me that there was an investigation going on and there were witnesses to the accident. I went numb at the thought of me not being there to know what actually happened. As he began to tell me, I braced myself to relive Benjamins last moments. I did not know how my son died, part of me wondered if I really wanted to know. I had to know because these were the last moments of my son's life that I had missed.

The detective went on to state that a lady was coming down the highway headed toward him. He was trying to get over and out of the way, but she came over into his lane. This made him swerve to miss her. He drove into the ditch trying to avoid her hitting him. She never stopped. Even though he tried to avoid her, he couldn't. She was traveling too fast. She was in the hospital but would live.

I asked if it was possible that I could see her? I wanted to ask why she did not see him? and what had happened? The detective told me, "It wouldn't do any good. She could not remember anything. He had visited and asked those same questions. She did not remember seeing a car or hitting one. She was on medication while driving. Then he told me something that made my heart sick; her name was Linda, and somehow knowing that made me weak. I thought this is something else that I have to get over.

Benjamin's accident got the attention of the local news. There was no way that I could watch it, and still cannot to this day. A news reporter visited me after I came home from saying goodbye to him. The detective came to see me at my job again and stated that charges would be brought against the driver. I told him I did not know if I could do it, but he stated it was not up to me. Charges had to be brought, but he did want to know when I wanted them to pick her up. I could not make that decision at that time and told him that. I kept thinking about her family.

Her family members came to Benjamin's visitation. I was surprised to see them, and it was a nice gesture but not expected. I hadn't even realized until they walked in that I knew them. I had been doing business with them, even working with them when they came to my place of employment. We had even shared some church services together. It was as big of a shock to me as I know it was to them. Before the accident I could talk easily to both of these sisters. When I found out about the connection to them, it changed our relationship. Even though I did not plan it, in the back of my mind I blamed them too.

I felt scared, rushed, frustrated, and overwhelmed because of all of the decisions that were supposed to be made. I thought my God, "This decision I will make will affect so many, me, my family, their family. It would change things for the rest of our lives. I did not understand why it had to be a decision from me! Why was I the one that had to decide an answer for something that would affect so many. No one ever asked my husband anything or wanted to see him.

Lawyers were calling wanting to talk to us. I began to reflect on the fact and asked the Lord, "Will I ever be at peace again?" Things were happening so fast, and so slow. Part of me just wanted it all to be over. I didn't think I would ever feel whole again. I know there are always things happening that no one imagines; I was that someone that could not bring those thoughts to my imagination.

The detective continued to request a time for them to pick her up. They wanted me to commit to a particular time when they could pick up Linda for charges from the accident. I also could not imagine it. I felt like I would be turning her in, even though it was out of my control.

October came and the detective asked me again about a time. I told him to wait until after Thanksgiving, so she could have time with her family. He said he would do that. After Thanksgiving passed, I told him to wait until after Christmas. I did not want them to pick her up until after the holidays were over. In the midst of all of this my husband

and I had to go to court. It was another one of the hardest days of my life.

Sitting there and hearing questions asked, it was as if Benjamin died all over again. The only difference this time in my arms. Even though I could not stop the tears from flowing down my face. I know God had protected and shielded us both. I had not told my children about the authorities picking up Linda.

I was made aware that not even Linda would know if or when she would be picked up. There would be no advance notice given to her or her family. This was laying heavily on my mind. How could I knowingly place someone in this position? On the other hand, my son was gone, and she was still here. I was hurt, and upset, I felt that she had stolen and robbed me of my son.

I was contacted by the district court about making a victim's impact statement. This scared me, but my immediate thought was I'm not the victim! Or was I? Instead of making an oral statement they would mail papers to me. I had to write down how this crime had an impact on me and my family. I did not know if I could put into words how our lives had been impacted by the loss of Benjamin. It took weeks for me to write it, and all I still had to do was mail it back.

The day finally came when I was able to tell the detective, "Pick her up after the new year." I asked if they would let me know when it was done. I thought about the impact statement that was ready to mail. I know it would change the course of her life and could not understand how I felt good and bad about it. My life had already changed, and hers would never be the same again. But in the name of justice, a life had been taken, and a life would be given up.

I received a call from the District Attorney while I was at work telling me that I did not have to mail my Victim's Impact Statement back to them. She was at the courthouse, and I could bring it right over to her. On this very particular day I had brought it to work with me to take to the post office. I was so nervous when I heard those words. What would I do? Would I say anything when I handed it to them? What would they think after they had read it? Was I too harsh? Was I not harsh enough? What would they think of me?

Nevertheless, before I could leave my office, the detective was waiting to see me. They were going to pick her up, and I was not sure at that moment how I felt. What he said later, made my heart drop. Linda was rushed to the hospital and had passed away from a heart attack! I could not believe it! On a day like today when she was supposed to have been picked up. I was about to make them aware of what I had gone through. I wanted them to know how it made me feel. Now my baby boy's death will go unnoticed, and no one would be punished.

I closed myself in and forgot that my other children had lost their baby brother; my husband had also lost his baby boy. This pain and hurt was exhausting. I tried my best to hide it. I wasn't about to let anybody know just how I was really feeling. I had to carry it. I stopped letting anyone get too close to me. I became cold, hard, and dismissed others when they talked to me.

Why engage in a conversation? There was nothing to say. I didn't want to talk to anyone anyway. I can remember sitting there blank as people carried on a conversation by themselves. I wasn't listening. I just wanted to be left alone. Someone would say to me, "oh! You are going to make it." I began to wonder, "How do you know?" My life was like a pendulum swinging back and forth and I was barely hanging on.

Some people would say to me, "You are a Worshipper; you're going to make it. It's going to be alright. I'm praying for you!" What does that even mean? I'm going to be alright. Is that because of what I do or because you are praying for me? I can't worship! At that time, I had nothing to give God.

I didn't want to go to church, participate in church, or sing in church.

I can remember about two weeks after Benjamin's funeral, going to church one Sunday, I don't remember going inside. I had no idea how I had gotten there, but I was there. My body was at least. My husband was trying to hold things together while preaching, and I don't remember what he was preaching about. I had no idea who was there or even who talked to me. I do remember that I did not want to be there. I was mad at him for having me there. "I had to be there." People were not important to me at that time.

I could hear them say, "it's so good to see you." I would think to myself, "Who cares!" Did they not understand, "I don't care!" I just wanted to go home! I remember looking at the drums, Benjamin's drums, wondering why was he not there where he was supposed to be. It ate at me the entire time. There was all of the talking and hugging me. "If you need anything let me know." They would ask looking at me sad all pitiful and wanting to pray for me.

Everyone seemed to be talking except God. He wasn't talking. I began to ask God, "Why aren't you talking?" This became my clarion call, "Why aren't you talking God." I could not understand why God wasn't saying anything. It hurt so bad to listen to the silence. On June 22nd I woke up in the emergency room. Once again, I had no idea what had happened to me. I didn't know when or how I got there. Now I am usually a light sleeper, but obviously not this day. This is what I was told.

I didn't get up that morning with my husband before he left for work. He thought that was strange. The ambulance was called. I thought about how, the sirens and ambulance lights flashing on top of me not responding must have paralyzed him with fear. It was just weeks since we buried our son. I could only imagine how fear had gripped him. He showed me the marks on the frames of our doors that the gurney had made. I could not imagine what had happened. I did not remember.

I opened my eyes and saw my sister and my husband. They told me that other family members were in the waiting room. I still did not remember the ride to the hospital or anything else. I apologized to my husband for scaring him all while wondering if that was what death feels like. I wondered is death a vacant and nonexistent feeling. I wondered if Benjamin had felt that same thing on the day his car was hit by another vehicle. I said, "Lord, you allowed me to sense what it was like to die." The time that I was unconscious until I opened my eyes there was no fear; it was peaceful.

When I saw the doctor afterwards, he asked me was there any stress in my life, was I troubled or hurt over anything? I wanted to scream!! "Yes, I have lost my son recently and very suddenly, do you think that would cause any stress?" I found out later that the same ambulance driver that picked up my son on "the day" had also picked me up.

It was July 24, 2011 a little over a month before my son's 21st birthday which was July 30. God spoke these words to me, "DON'T BE UNGRATEFUL; JUST BE THANKFUL." Here I was sitting in church when the song; "Thank you Lord" was being sung. I did not realize it at the time until after God had spoken. God would not have spoken those words to me if I wasn't being ungrateful. Even in my time of mourning, He demanded his worship. He spoke those words to correct me. I got up out of my seat and I began to run around in the sanctuary.

I did not think about what was going on at the time or about what God said, I was just grateful that He said it to me! Later I realized that is why he had not been talking to me. I would not have heard him if He had. I was not in a position to hear. I had become someone I didn't want to be. I was mad at Benjamin for not being at home, for leaving me. I was mad at myself for not making him stay at home. I was regretting the things that I didn't tell him. I was wondering did he really know how much I loved him? I was angry at me for not being with him when he needed me the most. I was wondering what his last thoughts or words were. I was a total mess!

We live in a world where we want and search for an explanation for death. When death calls, we cannot handle something that each and every one of us has to face. God give us answers if we listen.

When I lost Benjamin that not only took something away from me and out of me, but who would have thought that I would also have to forgive. I was the one that was hurting and falling apart. Look what me and my family had lost. I felt that I was the one that had suffered and had to hold my feelings in and ignore everything around me that caused me to relive every moment that had been taken away.

I know it was a car accident, but I still recalled those words that God had spoken; "I could have, I needed you to see me." Little did I know just how much I had to give up and let go, and to know that because of what had taken place, forgiveness also had to come so that I could be healed. I had to admit, what I was holding onto, even if I felt that I had a right, so that I could be forgiven. I was going through emotions of denial, guilt, and blame. I thought if only Benjamin had not been on that road and stayed home.

I had not seen Linda's daughters in a while, and I was

okay with that. I did not want to face them, nor did I know what to say to them. I would see the older sister when I would go and take care of my bill and would welcome the fact that she would not be in the office when I would go there. The other would come to my place of employment to conduct business. My office was in the back, so I kept myself out of the way, so that I would not have to talk to her. I was afraid that if she looked at me, she would probably know what I would be thinking, even though I didn't really know myself.

One day I was left alone at the office. I was in a position of not being able to hide when she came in. I decided Lord, I'm going to handle this quickly as possible. I would conduct business and let her leave. I felt like I had to hold my breath for the entire time so as not to fall apart. Being that close to her brought back a memory that I was trying to hide.

The next week she came in again and there I was. I thought God what are you trying to do to me? You know I can't do this right now? I am trapped with nowhere to go and nothing to say. As I reached across the counter to receive what she was giving me, our hands touched. Neither one of us said a word. What we did was hold on to each other's hands without uttering a word. Tears flowed and little did I know that he had me right where I needed to be. I had to finally face what I had been running away from.

That day our tears did not only fall but our hearts fell and melted too, and it was the awakening of forgiveness that I needed to be open to. God could now show me who he was, and I could see me. Jeremiah 17:9 AMPC- *The heart is deceitful above all things, and it is exceedingly perverse and corrupt and severely, mortally sick! Who can know it [perceive, understand, be acquainted with his own heart and mind]?* We don't know what lies in our hearts, until it is tested.

I found out in communicating with her years later that she carried those same feelings of inadequacy, hurt and pain with her. She did not know how to approach me, or how to talk to me. We both felt a sense of blame. Healing took place on both sides, and when we saw each other, we embraced each other as sisters. I came to learn that Linda was not her mom, but her stepmom. And she could not understand why it affected her so much. I told her family is family!

I did not know that unforgiveness was in me. I had held on to that unforgiveness for someone that was gone on. I associated my pain and passed it onto them without even realizing it. If someone had asked if I had anything against them, I would have said emphatically "No!" They never did anything to me. Forgiveness is more than just a beautiful thing; it is also a healing thing. We are familiar with the words; if we don't forgive, we will not be forgiven; but unforgiveness can keep us from moving forward, and hearing from God.

Coming to Myself

"This is my baby boy!

"This cannot be happening, and it doesn't seem real or right."

"I know that I won't be able to handle this."

"I don't know how to simply let go because I cannot pray. I cannot worship. I can't even smile. As a matter of fact, I will never smile or laugh again. I'm not a psalmist. I'm just a mother that has lost her son, and whose life is torn apart."

When I saw Benjamin at the hospital, I expected him to wake up when I touched his face or called out his name. He did not open his eyes or say, "Ma!" All I could think of was that he was alone, and now I was supposed to leave him alone and go home. What made it worse was the long silent drive home from the hospital.

My husband, my oldest son and I, on a road alone heading somewhere we didn't want to be, home. There were people gathered together at our home that night covering us with embraces, prayers, and love. I would cry every time someone walked through the door. I felt like a fountain because of the tears that would not stop falling. Our home was overrun with people, yet I felt as if I was by myself. We all held hands. They prayed a corporate prayer, and I still did not feel any better, just pain! I felt a deep agonizing hurt that had grabbed me and would not let me go.

A funeral! Now I have to plan for something that is going to kill me even more. I have no idea how, but it all came together in spite of me. I went through it in a daze. Singing a song was impossible. I was not in any shape for anyone to lean on me. I wasn't asking, and God was not telling me what to do. I was drowning in my own despair. I didn't know what to do about it.

I wanted Benjamin's funeral services to be very special. I didn't really know what that meant. After all it wasn't something that I could keep from happening. The services on June fourth were beautiful. There was an overflow of people to greet and hug. They wanted to love on all of us. The weather, it was a clear, sunny, blue sky with fluffy white clouds. The clouds looked like they were so thick that you could lay on them.

Denial was still my friend. I didn't want to believe he was gone. As he lay there handsome in demeanor, and on his face was such a peaceful smile. "I kept thinking that Benjamin looked as if he was asleep." I know that he was not in any pain but what about me? I felt nothing but numbness; and I never knew you could feel nothing. My pastor Steve Jamison preached the word of God! Souls came to be saved and my husband and I were able to rejoice in the God of our salvation, and in Benjamin's salvation. I was able to dance before the Lord, praise in his presence and lift my hands.

At the cemetery, I looked up and saw his favorite orange and blue balloons were floating in the sky and I managed to say, "bye baby, I love you!" Later I thought about what had taken place; I was at home; I had eaten something; beautiful flowers lined my porch. People had brought lots of food. Prayers were being offered up for our family. There were hugs from so many, visits, and phone calls. How was I going to sleep? My son was in the ground.

I went back to the cemetery on Sunday just to see if it was all real; He didn't call home that night and say, "I made it safe Ma!" As he always did when he got to work or call when he got ready to leave work and come home. I was lost and no one could help me. I was dying and didn't know how to tell God. We kept looking at and driving over that same place in the road where the accident had happened, week after week on our way to and from church. It was like a bullet penetrating my heart through and through. I didn't see a need to celebrate a holiday. My daughter had to be deployed and left on October 4th the day before my birthday for Afghanistan. Thanksgiving and Christmas didn't seem important to me. It was as if they did not matter. I didn't want to cook. Now, I felt as if I had lost two of my children. I forgot that I had another son who needed normalcy in his life.

It was like having a fist clamped tight trying to hold on to something, but it kept passing through your hands. Then on December 18, 2011 we were on our way to an afternoon service at church. When we crossed the bridge, the Lord dropped a song in my spirit entitled "I Am Healed." I did not know at the time, but it would end up being the first song for a new album that God was giving me. In the midst of my suffering, he was ushering me into something that he already knew I was capable of doing. Yet, I could not see, nor did I want to.

One day while standing at Benjamin's grave; through my pain, tears, and frustration I began to talk to God. I have often heard people say that you don't question God. But I am his child, and he is my father. Therefore, I thought that I had a right to come to him. And I was coming to him out of desperation. 1 Peter 5:7 (AMP) *says casting all your cares [all your anxieties, all your worries, and all your concerns, once and for all] on Him, for He cares about you [with deepest affection, and watches over you very carefully].* Since the death of my son, I was at a place and I didn't have to go to it because I carried the place around with me every day, not realizing that one day began and another day ended, I was just, going through the motions and not trying to look lost when people looked at me, but I was not doing a good job at that. His death was eating away at me and taking on a disguise that looked hurtful as well as unrecognizable.

This was a distant place that was also in and through me, which felt as if I wasn't even alive. It was as if someone else was living my life and I was on the outside looking in. It is so easy to hide in that place; you don't have to touch anything; you don't have to come in real contact with anything or anybody. You don't have to be a part of anything. You don't have to feel anything or really respond to what's going on around you. That's the way I felt. My life was dismal, gray and dull. I was unattached, separated from everyone and everything.

I thought somehow that was comfort and that I felt a sense of solace. Actually, I felt nothing. Looking at his headstone I began to meditate, and I ask God three questions, but I wasn't even sure if I was ready for an answer. He answered and the answer led to this book. This book opened my eyes.

Healed: My Journey

How Do I Make It?

The strength within!

"DRAW ME NEARER"

The Past (Behind us but not forgotten by us)

"God what strength? I don't feel strong." I could not feel anything, and what I once thought I had was already long gone. All I could think of was the memories. If this is what I have to keep me and help me make it through it wasn't enough. All those things that should remind me of what a special time together we had weren't working. They were not just memories. They were and are Benjamin's life and mine.

For me, the strength would come in the form of a dream, smile, or laughter that we shared. A phrase that he used to say, a scent in the air that would remind me of him, favorite food, a song, his favorite colors, or just the way he would say Ma! These are things that strengthened me. I would say, "God please don't let me forget what these things feel or look like."

God allowed me to understand that was not it. There was more strength required and I didn't have it. Every Wednesday and Sunday we would drive over the tire marks and painted lines on the highway. Seeing those places in the road were like staring down a very dark bottomless hole. My tears were there flowing into it and filling it up. The day his phone rang and called home at 2:51 to say goodbye before anyone else could call, reminded me that the strength I needed to survive was not on the inside of me. It had to come from God

The strength within was not my strength. It went so much deeper than the surface. It had to be placed inside of me. Isaiah 40:31 AMP - *But those who wait for the Lord [who expect, look for, and hope in Him] Will gain new strength and renew their power; They will lift up their wings[and rise up close to God] like eagles[rising toward the sun]; They will run and not become weary, They will walk and not grow tired.*"

When the Lord showed this scripture to me, I looked at the words. They said to me that I had to be taught to trust in the Lord again, in a renewed way. I asked for help. I had to get up, move, and prepare, so that I would know how to wait on him. It became my prayer and eventually a sermon. Lord teach me how to wait. If I was to gain strength within, I had to know how to get it. I had to know how it was going to work for me. I seem to be stuck. But I found out that I was just where I needed to be.

March 19, 2013, I heard the Lord say my name. He didn't call me to remind me that he knew who I was. He called my name out loud, so that I could hear him from the inside out. It was to remind me of who he was. He had gotten my attention and therefore he was not just calling me for nothing. It was personal, not just as one of his children, but a child that was also in need of their father.

I didn't have enough sense to be afraid. I just knew that if he had called my name, he had something to say to me. I had to prepare myself for what was next. It didn't take long. Five days later, March 24, 2013, God spoke again in the center of my pain when I thought that I could no longer hurt. "I could have! I needed you to see me." I cried out bellowing, for at that moment I didn't know what else to do. There was a confidence towards God, and somehow, I knew that through that believing cry and those words that God was in charge.

Hebrews 11:27 (AMP) *remembering like Moses, By faith he left Egypt, being unafraid of the wrath of the king; for he endured [steadfastly], as seeing Him who is unseen.* I had seen the unseen, and it was not that my eyes had not been open. I saw him from a different perspective, through the eyes of the Spirit. I didn't just see things with a different frame of mind, but with a different spirit myself. Everything I had seen before was clearer. God was allowing me to see him and the move of his hand.

One day I was walking, and I looked up. I saw how beautiful the sky was. It was like the picture-perfect day of Benjamin's burial. I called it a Benjamin day! I began to look at the sky. I took off my glasses, put them back on and repeated the steps. I saw the orange spots in the sky all over on top of the clouds. I knew that Ben was right there. It was as if I could feel him and see him smile, floating on the clouds.

God was so gracious that he allowed me to see a portion of his glory. I felt so close to God. I started to not just look to him but look for him. I learned that the strength within that I needed had to come from God. He showed me and gave me moments in my life from my son that strengthened me too, and no one else can take them away.

I would have dreams. I would hear and see him play the drums. The sky opened up to me, and God showed me just what he could do. One particular dream that I treasured happened on December 11, 2011. Benjamin was sitting in a car with other young men, it was a white Cadillac convertible with three in the front and three in the back. He looked so handsome, and I knew he was in the care of someone else. It was as if he didn't really know but yet he knew.

He got out of the car. I was sitting down on a bench on the curb. It was a blue bench, one of his favorite colors. He saw me and the driver stopped. Benjamin was sitting in the back seat in the middle. He didn't ask anyone to open the door or move. He just jumped over the other person he sat next to and came to sit beside me on the bench. He laid his head on my lap. I was so glad to see him. I was crying so hard; and tears were streaming down my face. I told him that I thought he was gone. He replied, "I'm not gone Ma, I'm just floating on a cloud!"

God knows that next Sunday we were on our way to church and the sun was coming up. I was looking through the windshield as if I was looking for him. My husband asked me what I was doing on this beautiful day. An array of orange and blue colors on a beautiful horizon met me, and what an awesome sight. It was as if heaven had opened up. I couldn't help but shed tears for what God had shown me. From that day on, I began to look at what I couldn't see with my natural eye, and trust God for that strength within that I did not believe or know I had.

The very next week I went into a store, and I saw the little blue bench in my dream for sale. I didn't even ask how much it was. It was there for me, and although I had read this scripture before, I was just now experiencing it. Psalm 46:1-3 (AMP) *God is our refuge and strength [mighty and impenetrable], A very present and well-proved help in*

trouble. Therefore, we will not fear, though the earth should change And though the mountains be shaken and slip into the heart of the seas, Though its waters roar and foam, Though the mountains tremble at its roaring. Selah.

My earth was shaking, and the mountains had already fallen down. The strength that I needed was God. His strength: not mine, because I could not survive on my own. I had to cry out to God, not just for what I thought he could do for me, but to hold me. I needed to hold on to him with all my might, and then everything else would be found in him. I had to know just who he was and not for everyone else, for me.

In January 2012, one Wednesday night we were on our way to Woodland to bible study, and I passed out. The last thing I remembered was that I was singing in the car, and when I knew anything else it was the next day. My husband told me that he had driven as fast as he could while Jon continued to call my name and hold up my head. I went limp.

The next day I remember getting up out of the bed with pajamas on and it was the middle of the day. My brothers had come to see me. Oh My God! I now know that I have to trust you for healing in my physical body. It had happened again. God had spared my life. I thank God today for his plan and purpose for my life, and even more for him speaking life into my dark place. I knew where my help comes from.

The doctors could not explain what had happened; but the Lord was not only my help, but my only hope. I felt like I didn't have anything to lose. I remember God brought to my spirit 2 Samuel 12, when David's son died; David wept, prayed, and fasted to God for a week that his son would get well. He didn't get well; he died. The servants were afraid to tell him. but when David found out that the child was dead, he realized that there was nothing more he could do himself but live. No matter what he wanted, his son was gone. David would see him again one day, but God's will had been done.

His son could not come to him, but he would be able to go to his son.

When God placed this scripture in my spirit it was March 4, 2015, and I called it my release date. God released Benjamin in my spirit, and I started to see something different. Benjamin could not come to me, but if I continued to live my life the way God required, I could go where he was. I know this to be true for myself. 2 Corinthians 12:9 *but He has said to me, "My grace is sufficient for you [My lovingkindness and My mercy are more than enough -- always available--regardless of the situation]; for [My] power is being perfected [and is completed and shows itself most effectively] in [your] weakness." Therefore, I will all the more gladly boast in my weaknesses, so that the power of Christ [may completely enfold me and] may dwell in me."* (AMP)

I thought that I would have to use everything that I had down on the inside of me to keep going. I needed something to go along with God's strength. I had to find out that God knew what I had and that was nothing! I was not able to give anything. That did not seem right, to rely totally and completely on him. I needed to give him something back. I didn't want to just give over and let him have me along with the problems that I had, the pain, the hurt, the agony, the fear, the disappointment, the anger, the coldness, and the misunderstanding.

To think that I could actually give God all of me and this too and he would do everything else! This was unthinkable; I had to let go of all the deep set hurt that someone had taken my baby away from me. I would have to do some forgiving. I had to admit my part in this too, in order to receive just what I needed, forgive so that I could be forgiven. I had to learn that you can't place blame on someone or something that happens when it is God's will.

It was amazing that God supplied strength when I wasn't expecting it or looking for it. Before I knew anything it was already there. He allowed me to see that the strength that he was freely giving to me was not for a particular season, but I could rely on it being there if I stayed in him, he was and is the strength. I began to wonder about the strength within that I would need to get through grief, mourning, depression, and fear and even trying to live life itself. God's strength didn't come by itself, without some realization; there was something that I would need to go along beside the strength within and that was the power to move out of the way and let God do it. I wanted to fix things, but I didn't have the ability or know how.

I had to learn to give up and recognize that I couldn't,

which was a hard thing because I had to actually admit "God I can't do it, and God I can't see it, but deep down it's there somewhere," I give up! I love the way Hebrews 11: 1(AMP) says; Now *faith is the assurance (title deed, confirmation) of things hoped for (divinely guaranteed), and the evidence of things not seen [the conviction of their reality--faith comprehends as fact what cannot be experienced by the physical senses]*.

In other words, in order to really have faith we must be sure of what we really hope for. At the same time be sure of what we can't see. I couldn't see what I really wanted, but I trusted in him, the only one that could bring it to pass. God granted me grace and patience, yet the strength within me was no ordinary strength, because I didn't have to depend on me, this strength was the supernatural power of God that allowed me to stand, and I thank God that I wasn't required to do it in my own strength.

How Did I Get There?

The joy of the Lord is my strength!

"HIDE IN YOU"

Present (Here with us and Now)

Psalm 118:24 AMP-This [day in which God has saved me] is the day which the Lord has made; Let us rejoice and be glad in it.

Good morning God!

Good morning Jesus!

Good morning Holy Spirit!

Good morning Ben!

Hi Ma!

God, I thank you, for waking me this day, Lord, I praise you for being who you are, you are my God! My Strength, my Savior, my Redeemer, my Source, I bless your name and I honor you. God, I thank you for this day that you have given me. This is the day that the Lord has made, and I agree with your word, that I shall rejoice and be glad in it; not just the day, but the one who made the day. I magnify you, Lord for you alone are worthy to be praised. You alone are awesome; you alone are worthy of all the glory and power that is due unto your holy name.

Nehemiah 8:10, says *for the joy of the Lord is your*

strength and your stronghold. The focus that I need is found in the joy. This joy is not made up, because it's not about me; I have to reach out to the Lord and everything that he has. The agenda that I need is his agenda, his purpose, his plan. It's not about increasing my own joy or mission, if I am able to do or live the way God wants me to, then this is the way that I become stronger, by doing his will. I have to remind myself that God is real and approaching him in a real way.

The joy that the Lord gives me makes me strong and has nothing to do with what I have but who lives through me and how I allow my life to be led by the joy; My true strength is led by the joy, and no one else can take that away from me unless I give it to them; for it is always there, we just don't recognize it. The joy that I experience becomes a knowing that I don't have to do this alone, the joy that the Lord gives is not about gladness, because it supersedes emotions, likes and dislikes; I'm finding out that I can get to a place of joy in God even when there is hurt.

Joy is about the pleasure that I have in God, and not based on my feelings. God's joy helps keep me sustained but yet I know that getting to that place was nothing but the grace of God, if it had not been for the Lord, I would be somewhere sitting in a corner rocking and wearing a hug me coat. But I still look for Benjamin and I expect to see him, because of what has been birthed in me from crying out to the Lord. I still shed tears, but they are not the same tears, because there are times when I can see his smile and sense his laughter. I still miss him not being here in the natural, yet I'm learning to see and experience something so much bigger, a relationship with God, and joy that I never knew before, and that relationship is allowing me to be close to my son just by being close to God. That same joy gives over to Praise, and spills over and out of me and it can out of you too. It came together for me, the more I praised, the more joy I had, and the more joy I had the more I wanted to praise.

When establishing a relationship, it's not just about coming before God (the creator), thanking him for Jesus (our savior) and The Holy Spirit (our guide), but it is the closeness of a friend that is for us. I began to praise and worship him, without trying to gain something from him, I knew that, and I still know that Linda was created to praise and worship him. I come before him closing everything else out and everybody; I tell him who he is, not for everyone else or the opinion of others but whom he is to me. I begin to pray when I get up early, and one day the Holy Spirit reminded me of when I was a child, and we would play tag and, in the game, whenever you got to someone else you would touch them and say you're IT! We would run and tag one another, and that person became IT! My tag time has become my "Time Alone with God"! When we touch God, he will touch us back! I can touch him again and again, and I found out he will always touch me back and that he loves for us to long after him. When we played the game, being IT was very important, even though we wanted to be IT and at the same time we didn't want to be IT but we had to look for someone other than ourselves. When playing the game nobody lost because it was fun, challenging and we ran.

God reminded me that the strength that I gain during my tag time is priceless and different every day, because no matter what I keep pursuing after him. I used to think that getting down on my knees in prayer was the only way to open myself up to God, but I love the open spaces that he has taken me too. Today I know how important a prayer life is but equally also a praise and worship life, I thought that's what I was doing before, but now I feel that I actually have a better understanding, but even though I get it wrong sometimes by not praying as I ought and communing with him.

I thank God that my strength is not measured by how many times I give up. God is showing me who he is in so many ways, I can walk down the road and see him in the simple things like a flower, in a blade of grass, in water, and even in the sky and praise him for who he is and thank him for allowing me to see him just as he promised. I love seeing God in areas that I never expected and knowing that I can yet spend time with him and can catch smiles with Benjamin at the same time. God led me to listen not just with my ears or just seeing him with my eyes wide open but also with my heart and knowing how much he has given me; this led me to an amazing discovery of him and placed in my spirit revelations and that is how I began writing "Message from The Clouds".

I not only just started to write it, but it speaks to me, to look for him and too him, about having an encounter that takes me far past who I expect to find. Somehow the struggle, the hurdles, and climbing up out of the rough place where I was and even coming from the mountains into the valley are not as deep and as wide as I thought until God raised me above them and my focus changed. I can look now and see where I once was, and I no longer am the same person.

Praise strengthens me for this journey, lifts me up as I lift him up, and magnifies who he is to me rather than what's wrong. Praise gets me up and uplifts me even when I feel at my worst, and I'm able to look beyond myself. Psalm 9:1-2

(AMP) I will give thanks and praise the Lord, with all my heart; I will tell aloud all Your wonders and marvelous deeds. I will rejoice and exult in you; I will sing praise to Your name, O Most High. Praise expresses our adoration, and that's why we should tell God how much we adore him. Praising God has nothing to do with how I feel, the feeling doesn't have to come before I praise God, praise is in order because God is worthy of it. I find that praise gets me out of the way and takes the focus off of me. The more that I praise God, the more I want to, it has helped me through so many times when I felt like I could not make it. And I thank God today for the power of praise in the midst of all the storms and in the middle of all the battles.

I love Psalm 34:1-2 (AMP) *I will bless the Lord at all times; His praise shall continually be in my mouth. My soul makes its boast in the Lord; The humble and downtrodden will hear it and rejoice.* It is impossible to set your heart to praising God and be sad, because it will uplift you and others around you. Now worship adds something that is different to me, because worship starts with a love for God. When I approach worship, it is something that God created me to be, and not just for something that I do, it becomes a lifestyle! I am finding out that there is more to me than writing a song, or singing about praising him, I thank God that he wants me!

not the song, not what I have heard from someone else that I may sing but he came for me! He sent his son to die for me, I am the song no matter what I sound like, because no one else can worship God on my behalf like I can, or you can.

John 3:16-17(*AMP*) *For God so [greatly] loved and dearly prized the world, that He [even] gave His [One and] only begotten Son, so that whoever believes and trusts in Him [as Savior] shall not perish but have eternal life. For God did not send the Son into the world to judge and condemn the world [that is, to initiate the final judgment of the world], but that the world might be saved through Him.* My worship (me) is what I have to offer up to God that I cannot copy from no one else. I know there are people that God have placed in my life to pray for me for real, and I thank God for having intercessors standing in the gap for me, even when I don't know how to look out for myself, but I also value the anointing and understand how important it is because flesh begat flesh and Spirit begat Spirit.

By staying in God through his word, and being connected to him, that strengthens me from the inside, and it has to be more than just a connection, but a relationship. The strength of the Lord builds me up on the inside so that I can live this life. God also gave me strength through an avenue that I did not expect, because I didn't feel that I could function as a praise and worship leader, but healing came through the album, that God allowed me to write songs for, I didn't intend to do another one, but I thank God that the strength he gave was so much greater than the pain; through "Celebrate God," I envisioned what God had become to me, I experienced him in a way that I have never experience him before, in surrendering myself and just giving over to him, instead of giving up and dying. They became my songs of praise, along with a call to worship.

Today, even though Benjamin is not here in the physical, that does not keep me from communicating with him, because he's always with me, there are days that I may not have anyone to give me a hug or hold my hand when I start to feel a little sad, but God holds onto my heart; yet when I think of him, it's with a smile, a joy, and I can see him smile, telling me Ma, I'm alright, don't cry, I become stronger because of the strength of the Lord. Lord, I can't hide from you, but I can hide in you, in your comfort, your peace, and in your forgiveness.

Where Do I Go from Here?

"CELEBRATE GOD"

The Future (Tomorrow and any day we have not seen)

Hebrews 12: 2-3(AMP) [looking away from all that will distract us and] focusing our eyes on Jesus, who is the Author and Perfecter of faith [the first incentive for our belief and the One who brings our faith to maturity],who for the joy [of accomplishing the goal] set before Him endured the cross, disregarding the shame, and sat down at the right hand of the throne of God [revealing His deity, His authority, and the completion of His work]. Just consider and meditate on Him who endured from sinners such bitter hostility against Himself [consider it all in comparison with your trials], so that you will not grow weary and lose heart.

God gave me these two scriptures; and I know that I can't give up. I don't go backwards! I can't afford to go backwards! I have to keep my eyes focused on Jesus because that's where my faith is. (This is one of the answers.) What God has allowed me to do is pick up my bed and walk. I'm reminded of a song my mother would sing now, "where shall I go but to the Lord."

When I was called into the ministry, God gave me my assignment in Isaiah 61, when he told me to comfort all who mourn, and I thought, "this is impossible to do when I need comforting myself." But in comforting others I am being comforted.

So, this is what I am to do for others in the area of the ministry, giving comfort through whatever God allows me to do in order to pass on the joy of the Lord, and the strength; even in this, he helps me to continue on. Philippians 3: 13-14 (AMP) *Brothers and sisters, I do not consider that I have made it my own yet; but one thing I do: forgetting what lies behind and reaching forward to what lies ahead, I press on toward the goal to win the [heavenly] prize of the upward call of God in Christ Jesus.*

God is real. The future is real. Because God desires that none should perish, and that we all have a right to the tree of life, my hope is in him. I keep my praise and the joy that the Lord desires for me, keep looking up, as I live this life that God requires, for me to be a witness for him and not just with words and deeds but also actions and with my lifestyle. I have said that I didn't want to be a person that bothers anybody, but I do; bother someone if it is going to help them, care about them just that much as the Lord leads because God has given me life, I have to show others what life actually looks and feels like, and he has also given me instructions to follow in his word.

He is my perfect example; I am to live my life to reflect the life of Christ; and in order to do that I have to bother someone else. It may put a demand on someone or make someone's life change for the better. I don't want to just be the kind of person that talks an example but not live it. I want my life to reflect righteousness. God is coming back after a church, and I want to be part of the church here on earth that God comes back for. To be with him to the place that he has prepared for prepared people.

Benjamin still speaks to me today in so many ways, and I thank God. Even more so I thank God for granting me and showing me how I can sense the glory of his divine presence. The sweet aroma of his joy, the power of his strength and the protective guidance of his hand. I love 2 Timothy 4:8 (AMP) In *the future there is reserved for me the[victor's] crown of righteousness [for being right with God and doing right], which the Lord, the righteous Judge, will award to me on that [great] day-- and not to me only, but also to all those who have loved and longed for and welcomed His appearing.* The word of God gives me hope, not just for the future, but for eternal life, and I can have it in him. [We say that death should not be feared by the born-again Christian but, we have something to fear, if we have not prepared for it. I don't know of a single person that does not want to go to heaven, but we forget that there are stipulations, and we fail to get ready, so we are not prepared.

I'm not going to tell anyone that as time goes by, that your pain does too or you stop hurting but it does become more bearable, I will forever miss my son and some say that time heals all wounds, but it doesn't; it's just that the time allows us to process it; you get better because prayerfully you become better over time processing in the Lord and with the strength of others. I am not the same person that I use to be, and I thank God that I am not, because I would not have made it, I died too and at the same time became free from negativity that was brought on by myself and others. Today even though I can pray, visit the grave site, and talk to Ben; I also have to continue to commune with God through praise, worship, reading his word meditating, preaching, and singing and having fellowship, and all of this strengthens me for this journey. No, I never thought that I could be grateful for my past, able to rejoice in my present while preparing for my future. Benjamin is healed, and so am I.

Goodnight God!

Goodnight Jesus!

Goodnight Holy Spirit!

Goodnight Benjamin!

Goodnight Ma!

In Memory of Benjamin Daniel Lane

Special Acknowledgements

I send a special acknowledgement to my boyfriend, my love, God fearing teaching husband and love Thomas. He was holding my hand every step of the way and encouraging me as I walked down this road.

To my three extraordinary children Crystal Qiana, Jon Robert, and Benjamin Daniel; to my beautiful daughter who has always believed in me. She reminded me, "When someone ask what you're doing, say that you're building an empire." Thank you for backing me up and believing in me.

Jon Robert, you helped me when the right words couldn't seem to come to surface. You didn't always know what to think or how to feel about what was happening. By faith you trusted the process and stood by my side.

To Benjamin Daniel my baby boy I know you hear me, because you are the reason for me seeing what I see through your eyes. God allowed you to walk through and down this road with me. Thank you! It was through your eyes that I have been able to see God who is no longer invisible.

I thank God for wonderful parents the late Robert Lee and Lucy Mae Raleigh who gave me life and the ability to be who I need to be. You raised me up in the fear of God. My brothers and sisters; big brothers Robert and Lee (who are like my daddy). They let me know that I am more than just a little sister. My big sister Dorothy, (like mama) even when she wasn't trying to be. The best sister that I could ever ask for. I thank God for the closeness that we share, not just one of siblings but friends.

To the rest of my family, I'm glad to be a niece, an aunt, and a cousin to so many special people; Raleigh, Bowens, and Townsend.

I appreciate my sister Evangelist Velma Ledbetter for speaking into my life when I was in a low place. God allowed her words to take root in me. Thank you for your encouragement without judgment. Evangelist Gloria Jamison, my mentor, teacher, and instructor, always demonstrated the power of God before me, and speaking to me even when I wanted to let go.

I am so grateful for my Pastors the late Steve Jamison and Loren Jamison for the foundation that they placed in my life and lived before me. They were always preaching and teaching the word of God, praying, and giving me Godly counsel. Bless you both for showing me the power of prayer.

I want to send love to a friend Minister Doris Gathings, who saw ministry in me when I couldn't see it and refuse to see it myself. For Pastors Michael and Sharon Cannon, thank you for carrying me to the altar, shouting out my name and having spiritual communion with me.

My church family Palestine M. B. (Mighty Baptism) church, your love and support mean so much to me! I love you all so much. To Special friends, Pastor R.H. and the late Bettye Brown. Thank you for inspiration and fellowship. Bless you for letting me know that you believe in me and that I can do it.

Pastor Donald and Barbara Page God bless you! What can I say, you have no idea what the coffee did for me; I love you both. You fed us when we didn't know we needed to be. To my brother and sister in the Spirit; Michael and Cynthia Jefferson there were days that you carried me over. There were days you carried me through, and you gave me something to pour into. I thank you for (Grace for the moment).

To one of the best armor bearers the late Brenda K. Gates, thank you for your letters, cards, uplifting hugs, and all that she did for me; to Pastor Norman, and Mattie Jamison, you both act like my uncle and aunt. I love you both for showing me that I can just be me and still be accepted. (Sis. Mattie thanks for the advice).

Healed: My Journey

www.ingramcontent.com/pod-product-compliance
Lightning Source LLC
Chambersburg PA
CBHW041130110526
44592CB00020B/2756